"It might just be a Sunday afternoon in the suburbs, and you might just have taken a swallow of a particularly delicious beer at just the perfect temperature, and you are sitting in the most right, comfortable spot with just the right mix of sun, shade and temperature and in that one immaculate and perfect moment everything drops away. The world is just you and this one second that is the closest to perfect and eternity as you may get. That moment is a poem of the highest magnitude, and this book, Salt Holds No Secret But This, is full of those moments, those poems. These poems are moments acutely aware of their beginning and are equally precise in their awareness that these moments are ending."

-Jason Baldinger, *This Still Life* (co-authored with James Benger, Kung Fu Treachery Press, 2022)

"In his latest offering, *Salt Holds No Secret But This*, Steve Brisendine masterfully tackles big issues like death and pain. He expertly weaves Biblical allusions and concepts together with everyday experiences. For example, he plays with the prophetic concepts of foretelling and forthtelling. He refers to the "cloud by day" and the "fire by night" that guided the Israelites when they left Egypt. Yet he shows us his drunk friend passed out on the kitchen floor. Like e.e. cummings, Brisendine plays with punctuation (particularly the parentheses) to guide the reader through each poem. He reminds us that "wisdom knows both rules and when to stomp them into bits," and that "pain redeems." We come away with a "wordless hymn to the Architect of thorn trees and broken glass" that is both fresh and compelling."

-Beth Gulley, *A Sticky Note Alphabet* (Alien Buddha Press, 2021)

"As has been amply evidenced in his previous works, Steve Brisendine has the uncanny ability to put those unfathomable emotions which are germinated by the uncertainty of life into the perfect words. *Salt Holds No Secret but This* is no exception. If anything, it's a perfect example of Brisendine's skill in crafting the perfect poem to transport the reader to an exact moment. Something as deceptively simple as: "Summer/writes itself in/ rockabilly riffs and/termite scrawls/on a 2x2," gives the audience an instant front row seat in the concert of the moment. Deftly intertwining enviable word economy with relatable situations, metaphor, and depth, this book holds secrets that will only be unlocked through multiple readings. Brisendine warns us, "Art must go unmasked and contagious," and *Salt Holds No Secret but This* does just that, permeating the reader's consciousness with a truth rarely seen, and certainly seldom expressed. Be warned: as with all good art, after reading Steve Brisendine's latest, "There will be a scar.""

-James Benger author of *From the Back* (Spartan Press, 2020)

"On the cover of Steve Brisendine's book of poems, "Salt Holds No Secret But This", is the picture of a dilapidated shack. Brisendine knows poems are built, stack and pile, skeleton and skin, in a manner architectural, begun with words. When he asks the atheist, the agnostic, and the believer, "how does the green of my eyes taste?, we answer in unison like a bag full of souls. These poems do not allow the reader to look away easily - whether a reader wants to is a hard question they must answer for themselves."

-Paul Koniecki, *Terrible Grace* (Luchador Press, 2022)

Salt Holds No Secret But This

Poems by Steve Brisendine

Spartan
Press

Spartan Press
Kansas City, MO
spartanpress.com

Spartan
Press

Copyright © Steve Brisendine, 2022

First Edition: 1 3 5 7 9 10 8 6 4 2

ISBN: 978-1-958182-05-5

LCCN: 2022939588

Cover image: Jon Lee Grafton

Author photo: Alan Hainkel

Acknowledgements:

I am grateful to have been included in the publications where the following poems first appeared:

365 Days Poets Anthology, Vol. 3: "in all beginnings are the words," "Rootwork," "trading someplaces," "And Those Who Know Will Always Feel," "exit and epilogue," *Circle Show*: "Second Sunday, 34th Year," "chase," *Review*: "Oracles and Vessels," *Book of Matches:* "Subsurface," "Sprawlville," *Gasconade River Review*: "tongues of flame in the house of God," "Phantom," "Shine and Show," *As It Ought To Be*: "Working Out a Splinter at Three O'Clock on Good Friday Afternoon," "Pickling," *Squawk Back*: "track 2," "Overnight Lows," *Flint Hills Review:* "Carniceria y Restaurante," *Rushing Thru the Dark* (Choeofpleirn Press, 2021): "High Planes," "The Boatman and the Queen (finalist, 2021 Derick Burleson Poetry Prize, "*Aji*: "signs behind the times," *Speckled Trout Review*: "To the Last Enemy, Upon His Brief Victory," *Rye Whiskey Review*: "Pint, Pipe and Ramble," *Dead Peasant:* "closed season," *Grand Little Things:* "January Mummer," "Finale," *Connecticut River Review:* "Divinations,"

In addition, "Thorn" and "Open Letter to a Synesthete"were featured in "Synesthesia" (2011), an exhibition of poetry-inspired paintings by Jennifer Rivera at Apex Art-Space in Kansas City, Mo. "Delta Days" was created and recorded on YouTube for VALA Gallery's "Convergence" art event (2021), both online and at the George Schlegel Gallery in Roeland Park, Kan.

Thanks are due to all of these folks:

To James Benger, Dan Pohl and the late Diane Wahto, editors of the third 365 Days Poets anthology, who were the first to take my poetry under my own name;

To Jason Baldinger, Sara Minges and James (again), for giving the manuscript of this book a keen advance reading and providing invaluable suggestions;

To Allen Heinrich, Penny Thieme, Adelaide Crapsey, Denis Garrison, Dante Alighieri, Shawn Pavey, Brian Ferry and Midge Ure, for various forms (sometimes literal) of inspiration;

To John Cornett, without whose badly needed offer of home improvement work years ago the poems "Working Out a Splinter at Three O'Clock on a Good Friday Afternoon," "Sprawlville" and "Track 2" would not exist;

And most importantly, to my wife, Kerri, for not only putting up with but also encouraging and supporting this poetry thing.

-Steve Brisendine,
November, 2021

Table of Contents

For Samuel, whose spirit made the return trip

It is the glory of God to conceal things,
but the glory of kings is to search things out.

-Proverbs 25:2 (RSV)

in all beginnings are the words

by this you shall know,
when the talk meanders

from poetry to
Jesus to too much cheap red

(let he who is without shame
take a breather from

reciting cummings and be
the first to mark Jack's

outline with tape where he lies
passed out on the kitchen floor)

wisdom knows both rules
and when to stomp them into

sharp glittery bits --
only for affect, not for

affection; couplets care for
far more than coupling,

and truth can find its way back
to a borrowed bed

under a Friday night sky
where all stars shine clear as grace

Second Sunday, 34th Year

Black-ink day for florists,
restaurants, regrets;

I have written decades' worth of
what I should have said then,
and still not touched the half of it.

If I crumple and put fire to each page,
sow ash just west of your headstone,

will words creep down roots of grass,
find their way into your dreams of
the New Earth,

of roses rising through
cracks in the bones of roads?

Delta Days

Policies, politics, opinions differ. Incentives are offered; consequences play out in crowded wards and funeral homes, in cries of *I wish they had...* meanwhile, we scribble and sculpt, brush and weave. Stories remain to be told, visions shown, dreamscapes mapped. Even if we must declaim at distance, even if rules limit beholding eyes to two at a time, ideas still find new hosts. Art must go unmasked and contagious.

> between trunks
> of the mulberry tree,
>   pink hibiscus

Oracles and Vessels

-after the artwork of Penny Thieme

I. Foretell/Forthtell

Each open grave
yawns a prophecy
of sated hunger.

The Earth means to reclaim
our dust; it grumbles
against breath and spark
and the thumping
persistence within
our rib cages –

systole of
        NOT,
diastole of
        yet,

auricles and ventricles
pulsing in defiance

(perhaps in denial)
(perhaps in
        Please, not today)
against proclamations,
foretellings and forthtellings
of beats slowed... stilled.

Whether slowly, after long seasons,
or with shattering suddenness,
fulfillment awaits.

II. Vessels Within Vessels

Here is a secret, whispered within our veins
and telegraphed along wires of nerves:

We are both container and conduit,
receptacle of life and the viaduct

along which it moves from generation
through generation through (re)generation,

and within these clay-walled vaults,
we carry the seeds of the second chance.

Subsurface

He is shot through,
he says,
with things that should not be
under anyone's skin.

The tingle and prickle
just west of his right shoulder blade
signifies, he is sure, the imminent emergence
of a tree
(elm, most likely) –

that, or one end of six yards or so
of string,
meandering in swirls and eddies
just beneath the surface of his back.

And when he thinks
of uprooting the sapling
in one wet
red
rip,

or of drawing out the string, inch by
half inch by
quarter
inch,

his eyes shine
with a *penitente's* joy.

> *Pain redeems,*
he says.

For now, he waits, meditates
upon roots and coils,
keens a wordless hymn to the Architect
of thorn trees and broken glass.

Thorn

I keep drawing blood
with this moot point.

It is no accident,
no careless pricking
of a hand thrust into
the pocket of a long-unworn
pair of trousers.

I put it into my shoe
and walk for miles,
past old churches
with red doors.

I often find myself
engraving

If …
into my eyelids,
so that when I blink,
I will not forget.

I take it to bed with me,
angled against my ribs
just so,

like a vandal's nail
carefully set
to puncture a tire.

tongues of flame in the house of God

I: the cloud by day

only some of the
smoke rises up to Heaven,

a grim billow of
red-letter King James *thees* and

thous and *thines,* of cabinets
and chairs and crayon

portraits of the Twelve; the rest
spills northwest, low to

the ground, shrouds my way (breathe in
Alpha, breathe out *Omega*)

II: the fire by night

neighbor-strangers line
Reeds Road, watch from upwind as

flames refuse to die;
we speculate cost and cause,

swap variations on a
theme of *I heard the*

helicopter, then sirens,
but I never smelled

any smoke (at home, dinner
is waiting, slowly burning)

Working Out a Splinter at Three O'clock on Good Friday Afternoon

You can't go easy, get the big bits out
and call it good –

not if you want it all gone,
not if it's buried, broken off
deep as the things that prick
at your dreams
when you sleep all the way through Saturday.

You have to keep at it until it all runs clear,
like there's water in the blood.

Then it's clean.

Then it's finished.

There will be a scar.

Sprawlville

Those who say they build houses here,
three rings or more removed from the city's heart,
guard secrets and sell a fable.

Stacks of lumber, pallets of brick,
portable toilets three degrees from perpendicular --
these are props, shuttled from site to site
to fool the uninitiated.

I once saw a man
with a map and a big beige bag of seeds
move through bare lots by moonlight,
sowing as he went:

Neo-Eclectic here, Prairie style there,
the odd Tudor Revival or Queen Anne
if the covenants permit such.

His humming sounded like every band
that ever cut its hair, sobered up,
paid for sensible imports and pleated khaki
with royalties from insurance-jingle ballads.

I do not know how strip malls get from
assembly line to busy intersection,
though I suspect they are dragged in
by teams of elephants,

feet muffled so as not to violate
noise ordinances.

The cul-de-sac itself
is actually a carefully bred species
of snake;

it rolls and stretches
to a prescribed length,
flattens out, locks smooth grey scales,
wills itself to die.

Those with decorative brick borders
down their sides
fetch more at market, but they are
also more prone to bite.

Unguided

Ante Meridiem, low single digits, in the suburbs:

There are no stars to be found
on these high overcast (past

mid-)nights, only a low grey/
white/grey ceiling and a glow of
       false dawn toward Downtown.

They are not hiding; they have
grown tired of competing with

our filaments and vapors, our
high beams and backlit menu
       boards and motion sensors.

The constellations have all
packed up and moved to the
country; Polaris (the last to skip
town) was supposed to leave an
       emergency supply of north,

but I guess she thought plotting
a course by working at right angles
from the moon would be enough --

and it might have been, but for clouds
moving in step/stop/start/step
        with each sleepless walker.

The last one still up and outside will
rule the parallax, set and re(re)(re)set

the rotation of the world with each
corner turned; the rest will wonder
        why their dreams slip, swerve, skid.

Track 2

Summer
writes itself in
rockabilly riffs and
termite scrawls
on a 2×2,

a loose
syncopated
thump of canvas
slip-ons tumbling
in the dryer,

the quick hiss-
pop of a nail
gun, a bird just
out of sight calling
             Marco ...

Mowing with Bryan Ferry
on a Pandemic Saturday

He showed up halfway through my second cut down the
        shrubline,
found me with earbuds in and volume cranked up against the
        motor's hum,
the hiss of somewhat-sharp steel through grass and (mostly)
        clover.

Even in sticky July air, he was tuxedoed and immaculate, hair
        falling
effortlessly just so, a magnet for lingerie and hotel room
keys arcing from the close-in rows.

I was sweating, though not the abandoned self-soaking of
almost four decades ago – the sort I'd get from dancing
        until three

with a stranger in a stonewashed miniskirt, and me with church
        in the morning.

I'd stand up, ghosts (never just one) of Tom Collins dawdling
down my spine, and mouth out

    To God be the glory, great things He hath done –

but now, this decades-on-from-vows now, it's inside to

clean up and put away groceries from the weekly face-covered
excursion;

her eyes roll, as they have for years, when I take a yard beer into
the shower.

I come out clean five minutes later with the empty,
knock something together from Friday's leftovers.

More than this, there's nothing,
he sang as I rolled up the lawnmower cord. He left it hanging;
was that, is that, will that be enough?

It is, and will be. We find old shirts to cut up for masks, plan
uses for a windfall of cheap scallions.

Evening now, and an Eighties cover band is playing online, a
virtual retro night out for fifty-plussers with nowhere but home
to be for another week.

No Roxy Music on the setlist, but – well, not just anyone can
pull that off, not even with backing tracks.

We dance until nine, with virtual church in the morning. I go
to hit the deadbolt, look outside, see him under the streetlight.
Tell me one thing,

he says, and leaves that hanging too. I shrug, smile, mouth
Now the party's over, I'm so tired
in response.

He slings his jacket over one shoulder, undoes his bow tie all the way, takes two steps and dissipates in a barely audible wash of lush synthesizer chords.

The Mennonite Girl Wearing Inline Skates
Plots Her Escape

She rearranges the baked goods, makes change for a twenty,
imagines her inevitable engagement to some still-faceless Levi,
            or Jacob, or perhaps Eli.

Then again, maybe she'll just dematerialize, ghost through
this folding table with its piles of pepperoni bread, its orderly
ranks of cinnamon rolls, its jars of wild plum butter,
            dandelion jelly, Queen Anne's Lace syrup.

There'll be no stopping her then; she'll take shape once more
and with three strong, sure sweeps of her legs, left-right-left,
she'll be off, gliding up and down rows of market stalls,
looking for some sunburned Travis, or Cody, or perhaps
            John David, arms harvest-hard under his T-shirt.

He will grin, look down and back up again, offer her
            a slice of watermelon.

She will meet and hold his eyes, bite deep, reach up
with sticky hands to unfasten her cap and free long hair
            long hidden from the world.

Open Letter to a Synesthete

Tell me,

> you who know
> the colors of B
> the letter
> and B the note,

whose palms are full

> of espresso,
> honey, wild
> plums,

who recognize the scent

> of a lover's voice
> over a thousand miles
> of cable …

tell me,

> how does the green
> of my eyes taste?

Rootwork

You can't tame a beet,
make a turnip elegant,
put an overpriced
sweater

(complete with sequins)

on a rutabaga and
call it *Fifi* or
Bitsy or *Princess;*

they're rough, stubborn
things that track dirt
into your mouth
and don't even pretend
at making sad
guilty eyes.

You have to give them
fat, smoke, salt,
rough treatment
with a heavy blade;
they'll come as
close to behaving
as they get.

Take that and call
it good.

ungathered

a fallen branch, black
walnuts scattered on the grass;

my mother's shade wakes,
raises one eyebrow, scowls at

my passing by this windfall
(Depression children,

even those gone to Glory
and its full tables,

are not content to let
the squirrels have their fill first)

Pickling

This acrid acetic sting goes beyond scent; it sets
hooks in your head, your eyes, your ideas about
$\qquad$ *enough*

and the cost of not having it,
like you're nose-to-nose with something wearing
your face, only with its curves sucked out –

jag, angle, pang, hunger hiding
$\qquad$ in cheek-shadows.

Fill, process, check lids, clear the table, spread towels:
this is monks' work, a bubbling clickclack chant
$\qquad$ of hands, tongs, glass, metal.

God of all perishables (one says
$\qquad$ *Father,*

but those who know vinegar speak first of
$\qquad$ *mother)*

preserve us against want, against waste, against
$\qquad$ burns and spills and shards.

Carniceria y Restaurante

I came here alone the day of
Tony's funeral

(he was always
asking before church,
        any menudo lately, hermano?)

now it's two of us, my son
and I, tucking into big bowls
of bright orange-red broth,
hominy, honeycomb tripe

(and knuckle -- makes the
whole thing richer, but you
have to mind the bones)

we pay our remembrances,
watch German football
in Spanish, try to puzzle out
whether what follows
is a variety show, a sitcom

or some hybrid involving a
renegade Capuchin monkey, a
studio audience and a
bad grey wig

I wonder if he'll come here
the day they lay me down

High Planes

You forget sometimes how
flat it is between river valleys,

how sky seals itself tight to prairie
no matter which way you look.

Then you get on a Panhandle
stretch of 54, between Hooker

and the Kansas line, and you see
why people used to think (or

maybe still do) that the planet
had sharp edges, void-rimmed.

This is why we put up our
steel juts and concrete jags:

wind turbines, grain elevators,
spray-painted water towers.

When they break the horizon,
we know there's a world beyond it.

signs behind the times

all the stones we have
        raised over millennia –

ziggurats, passage
        tombs, pyramids, megaliths –

in attempts to read our next
        chapters by the lights

above, when all of them speak
        to us from the past;

even the moon's pale advice
        arrives a second too late

To the Last Enemy, Upon His Brief Victory

For Emma Wales, 1917-2014

In the *iglesias Bautistas* of the meatpacking
towns, she was everyone's *Tia Emma*.

She shrugged you off for years, tireless
far beyond the allotted threescore and ten.

Two husbands, a son, two grandchildren,
a brother (my father, four years younger

to the day), her only sister: she knew your
grim hungry grin more than well enough.

She made you work for her, though, made
you break a bone-sweat under those robes.

You'd stagger up a dust cloud into some
village, sure heat and years had worn her out,

and find nothing but tire tracks out of town
and boxes of *Biblias Santas* left behind.

Did you read over a shoulder, see your
own demise written in the native tongue?
>   *Y el postrer enemigo*
>   *que será destruido es la muerte.*

Made the moment harder to enjoy, I would
think, when you finally caught her sleeping.

trading someplaces

morning fog carries
sound and conceals phantoms

or say rather that
it gives us ghosts' eyes, shades' ears;

this is how they take in our
world, this before-dawn

greyscape -- and how we will sense
theirs, walking shrouded

nightsinging streets from deathbeds
toward a creaking of gates

The Boatman and the Queen

-for Shawn Pavey

Charon has an Evinrude, bought
with the mouth-money of who knows
how many thousands of years' worth
of one-way passengers;

beats pole-work all to Acheron,
he says, and he still has enough coin
left over to swing the gas.

Sometimes, and don't tell Hades
this, Charon takes Persephone out
water-skiing on the Styx, way down
where the river runs still, dark, deep;

her hair flies free, like long grass
in a May breeze almost full-grown
into summer storm-bluster.

After, they drift at anchor, watching
his lantern glint off stalactites; she
tells him stories of rosebuds, of
new shoots on old grapevines.

He drops her off, kisses her forehead,
breathes in and holds the only scent of
pomegranate he will ever know.

Phantom

Streetlights
pass through me now;

so, too, strangers' glances,
the night-winds of
almost-spring.

I am a muffled chime,
bells wrapped in glass wool;

a crystal kaleidoscope filled
with shards of champagne flutes,
the dust of diamonds.

I am an echo of cat-feet
and Bradbury whispers
down streets where lovers walk,
dance in shadows,
dream themselves ghosts.

Crows no longer flap
and caw when I pass.

Their flat black eyes
can see the dead, but they do not
fear me.

Pint, Pipe and Ramble

I have danced with enough ghosts
already in this plague year.

Give me a glass of dark lager,
not memories, and let me drink
to my own company.

Let me taste the sweet burn
of phantom-free smoke, and
let ash be only ash.

Let my footsteps echo by ones,
my feet bear my own weight and
no other burdens.

There will be time and times enough
for all to mean more than itself.

And Those Who Know Will Always Feel

Why wait for the dead to
wait for the calendar?

The wall between now and Next
(life and Life, in other word)

is no thinner now
than in the kiss-instant
of a June wedding; ghosts sit with me

at tables for one, set the car radio
to memorial music, ride every forkful
from plate to palate.

Memento Mori is
Reveille and Taps,
on loop through all
times and seasons.

I know, I say. *I remember.* I mourn
against the advice of consolers,
and invoke my right to
their silence.

Cold Snap in the Osage Cuestas

These hills turn curved backs to the wind,
flat stone faces looking away southeast
to –

who can say? Not stones, nor grass, nor
corrugated sky with one rounded rectangle of
blue.

This was a seabed once; ammonoids still rest
here, brachiopods nestle between limestone
sheets.

Their years passed ages (*Pennsylvanian, Permian*)
ago; this year huddles, shivers, roars itself to
sleep.

Overnight Lows

The air has gone cold as a traitor's eternal bed.

Antaeus (he being the only unchained Giant
and *de facto* caretaker of the Ninth Circle)

has left his windows open again, and
wing-driven winds off Cocytus are
loose in the streets, howling reveled Hell.

They bear messages to be shoved under doors,
slipped in through tiny cracks in thick glass
and resolve.

I do not know what others might read,
whether warning or warrant or
denial of appeal –

but as to what comes to me, whispered
in snow-sibilants, I will not betray myself.

closed season

almost sunrise,
and Orion and his dog

still lurk overhead;
cottontails scatter into

the lingering dark at my
approaching footsteps,

though they have no more
to fear from me than

from the stars (not any more,
at least, but there was a time)

January Mummer

Almost
dusk, and something
flutters in dun grass -- one
dry oak leaf mimics a dying
sparrow.

Forging the Future

I was Destiny once, for a week
(well, for five days, anyway);
did I ever tell you that?

See, the horoscopes didn't come
from the syndicate as promised and paid for,
or maybe they got lost
in the shuffle of moving the newsroom --
and we had to do *something*.

Heaven – or the heavens – forfend
that the faithful should go without daily guidance,
tucked neatly next to bowling league scores.

Monday passed quietly enough;
the stars spoke through me in twinkling generalities,
advising perseverance, cautious optimism,
moderation in all things.

And I, King of Kismet,
orderer of the twenty thousand lives
in the greater circulation area, grew bored
and decided to stick a few baseball cards
in the spokes of the great cosmic wheel.
            Be careful,
I warned the Capricorns on Tuesday.
            Someone you trust is secretly plotting against you.

Wednesday brought this advice to the Libras:

> *That new relationship is all wrong for you;*
> *best to end it now and spare yourself the pain*
> *of long parting.*

The stars were most clear on Thursday,
concerning Taurus:

> *There's no better time to tell the boss*
> *exactly what you think, and don't mince words.*

The next week's horoscopes arrived on Friday;
finding myself suddenly under the sign of the lame duck,
I fired off one last celestial directive.

> *Confess that shameful secret,*
> the Universe whispered in the Leos' ears;
> *all will be forgiven.*

I tell this story now to a chorus of shocked laughter
and a litany of occasionally disapproving
variations on a theme of
> *How could you?*

> *It was easy,*
I say.
> *I just moved my fingers over the keyboard,*
> *like this.*

No,
they respond;

> *How could you do that*
> *to all those poor people*
> *who trusted you?*

Here, I can only shrug.
Someone had to take up the burden of Fate;
why not me – and why not have a little fun
with the job, especially at only two bills
for every sixty-hour week?

This response rarely satisfies.
They persist:

> *How could you be so cruel?*

Cruel?
Perhaps – but remember that I was Destiny,
an ambassador from the astral realm
with full diplomatic immunity.

Don't ask me how it all turned out.
I have neither humorous anecdotes
nor horror stories to share
about anyone who took my advice.

God might be omniscient;
I would have had to ask around,
and I never bothered.

He might care for those who follow His words,
but He had nothing to do with mine.

Besides,
If the sheep would choose a ram
(or a fish, or a scorpion)
for their shepherd, then let the flock
be bled and shorn and served up with mint jelly,
for all I care.

Me, I just work
for the newspaper.

Divinations

I: Rhapsodomancy
(*divination through interpretation of poems*)

Select, divide, parse until
lines on your forehead

outnumber those on my page;
the future does not

reside here, only such scraps
of the past as I

choose to disclose. Seek your
fortune (or fortunes)

elsewhere; all clues lead but to
even more riddles,

and words, nothing more, are the
rewards to be claimed.

II: Metoposcopy
(*divination through reading lines on the forehead*)

I can see and say my own sooth well
enough to decode patterns etched above

(or between) these two eyes:

> *He reads much, scowls in thought*
> *(or thinks in scowls) overmuch,*
> *needs to lay off or toss the salt.*

Expect these grooves to play
a soundtrack of the future, though?
I wish you luck with that;

they would not be there if I could look
as far as the next day and know
what to stand braced for.

III: Alomancy
(divination by the casting of salt)

Toss it, watch it fall. See the shapes
your eyes say it forms.

Burn it; observe its intensity,
the dance of orange flame.
All you will learn is that all things
move in cycles and waves.

Oceans rise, fall, dry to beds and flats,
rage at the strike of stones.

Salt holds no secret but this; our tears
always know the way home.

IV: Lithomancy
(divination by the casting of stones)

Gather and cast, in the proper turn;
Is this not what Solomon (perhaps)
and the song have instructed?

Do not misread between lines; only
on mountain roads and at the ends
of eras do falling rocks

act as portents (say rather as hulking
dutiful agents) of Fate. All else
is a wishful flinging, a flat

clatter of hopes and fears landing on
this unyielding truth: Stones will sooner
fall to dust than sing.

V: Abacomancy
*(divination by reading patterns
in the ashes of the recently deceased)*

> *Ashes to answers, dust to
> discernment,*

as though the pathways of life might
wind through the residue
death leaves in its wake –

Be careful, please,
we plead.
  Do not track my future
  across the floor;
  I have just swept.

Wind takes all, in the end,
and we are scattered by it.

VI: Austromancy
(divination by observing the wind,
especially the south wind)

No need to watch smoke, or bending of grass,
or the ten o'clock weather report;

Even on a calm day, not that those come often,
trees hunch toward the northeast.

This is the surest sign of what is to come, more
certain than any given in the heavens.

There will be hard southwest air, driving
clouds and tumbleweeds, fanning

lightning-struck tallgrass into crackling orange
curtains. This is the prairie's deep truth.

VII: Capnomancy
(divination using smoke)

Fire will consume all in the end, whether
falling from heaven or unleashed by men;
will smoke still waft through the air of
the New Earth?

We will have no call for signs by then, not
with eternity mapped out. Still, I hope that
there will be a need of poets.

Shine and Show

All that
we can do, we
who call ourselves poets,
is to carefully curate the
remains

of love,
of pain, of moments in their most
timeless forms, and put them
on display; sign
your name

upon
the paper, if
you must, but know this much:
that which you claim to own *(This is
my tongue,*

my hand,
my idea and no one else's)
is but held in common –
all the world's words
in yours.

chase

walk south all night or at least until
your ten-dollar sneakers give out
and you'll still never catch the moon
before the clouds take it

(probably best that way;
your garage is
full of junk
already)

Finale

Blue note
upon bent string
upon hushed interlude –
he leans back, eyes closed, and works dark
guitar

magic,
like he took shape at twilight and
has to blow town by dawn
with a bag full
of souls.

exit and epilogue

twenty years ago,
you died in my sleep on a

September Sunday
morning, a dictionary's worth

of words hanging unspoken
(or maybe unheard)

down hospital corridors;
I hope you gathered

my thoughts -- I still wake speaking
them sometimes -- on your way home

Steve Brisendine, a lifelong (so far) Kansan, lives and works in Mission, KS, where he spends much of his waking time trying to persuade words to line up and behave, with varying degrees of success. Occasionally, he does things with paint on canvas. He is the author of *The Words We Do Not Have* (Spartan Press, 2021). He has one tattoo and no degrees; that last part is his own fault. There's a good chance his pub quiz team is better than your pub quiz team, but you never know for sure about these things. Write to him at steve.brisendine@live.com.

This project was made possible, in part, by generous support from the Osage Arts Community.

Osage Arts Community provides temporary time, space and support for the creation of new artistic works in a retreat format, serving creative people of all kinds — visual artists, composers, poets, fiction and nonfiction writers. Located on a 152-acre farm in an isolated rural mountainside setting in Central Missouri and bordered by ¾ of a mile of the Gasconade River, OAC provides residencies to those working alone, as well as welcoming collaborative teams, offering living space and workspace in a country environment to emerging and mid-career artists. For more information, visit us at www.osageac.org

Osage Arts Community

www.ingramcontent.com/pod-product-compliance
Lightning Source LLC
Chambersburg PA
CBHW031255120626
46545CB00007B/2822